fresh start
BIBLE STUDY

my new
relationships
in Christ

debbie alsdorph

Victor® is an imprint of
Cook Communications Ministries, Colorado Springs, CO 80918
Cook Communications, Paris, Ontario
Kingsway Communications, Eastbourne, England

Fresh Start—My New Relationships in Christ
©2003 by DEBBIE ALSDORPH
My New Relationships in Christ is part of the
Fresh Start Bible Study Series.
Other titles include:

Fresh Start – My New Identity in Christ by Julie Baker
Fresh Start – My New Life in Christ by Nancy McGuirk

First printing 2003
Printed in the United States of America
1 2 3 4 5 6 7 8 9 10 Printing/Year 07 06 05 04 03

Senior Editor: Janet Lee
Editor: Susan H. Miller
Cover and Interior Design: Sandy Flewelling

fresh start
BIBLE STUDY

contents

introduction

The day you gave your life to Christ an exciting thing happened. Maybe you didn't notice it, but you changed. Scripture refers to this change as being born again. Often the term born again is reduced to joke material, for those who don't understand the power in the reality of being born again. Instead of referring to power, the idea of being born again gets reduced to some pathetic crutch or some insane obsession that crazy people called "Christians" hold on to.

Sadly, many believers also shy away from the realization that a new thing happened in them the day they received Christ. While hiding from the power of the truth, we become locked into believing in only a small God, rather than the big, mighty and powerful God he promises to be towards those who are his.

In this study we will look at what is different about our lives once we have committed to following Jesus. We will look at the solid truth of who he is, and how that relates to us in a real and personal way.

Most of us have heard the story of the old woman who died in near poverty conditions. Upon clearing her belongings from her one-bedroom apartment, her caretakers were shocked to find that she had over a million dollars hidden inside the boxspring of her mattress set. Over a million dollars!

Yet, this woman lived as if she was impoverished. She lived like a poor woman even though she was very rich. In the same way, many of us live impoverished as Christians. Our belief in God has not often touched the deepest part of us. Instead we live just scraping the surface of what God intended for us—as his own.

The best way to begin your walk with Christ is to sit with the basic foundational truths that are life changing. And, the best way to be re-energized spiritually is to sit with these same basic truths, until they re-charge your soul.

Are you ready?

But—beware—the caution on a package of batteries reads, "Caution—may explode or leak if recharged." And, I offer you the same caution today. You just might explode with new life, once you have been touched by the power of God's spirit. And, yes ... you just might leak Jesus on all who come in contact with you.

And—that is a good thing!

Let's trust God for a Fresh Start in all our relationships—beginning with Him.

connecting:

*our new relationship
with God*

B efore becoming a believer, I met a Christian woman who
was different than any of the others I had met. It wasn't
that she was perfect or all pulled together, but there was a
confidence about her that was attractive. After getting to
know her a bit better, I asked the million-dollar question, "So,
are you a real Christian?" She laughed at my question, saying
that no one had ever asked her that before. But I was serious.
I wanted to know if she had something genuine with God. I
was hoping she had something to offer me. After years of
being a church-going person, I was still empty.

I can remember the disconnected feeling of growing up
within a church without having a personal relationship with
Christ. Hearing the gospel of Jesus Christ had no impact on
the real issues of my daily life because I had not made a personal connection with Jesus. I had heard the message of salvation, but I hadn't opened the door of my heart to invite
Jesus in.

Now that I am saved, I've entered into the journey of
learning to walk with Christ. It's a daily choice. Personal surrender is not a one-time event. My new challenge is opening

up my heart daily to Almighty God in fresh surrender.

My emptiness wasn't the fault of a church. I faithfully filled a space in a pew but that wooden bench couldn't change my life! Church attendance could not bind up the broken places in my heart or set me free. Since my emptiness was coming straight from the inside of me—my heart—I had to discover a new relationship.

what is a relationship?

Relationship is: an association between two or more things; a connection, interdependence, link; a tie in, a hook up.

God, the maker of heaven and earth and all they contain, is a personal God. He is a relational God. He isn't so distracted running the universe that there is no time for us. In this lesson we are going to see how a relationship with our maker changes us. We will explore how the experience of this relationship gives us a desire to surrender and trust God.

Jesus came to set people free from the bondage of direction-less, power-less living. He came to empower, heal, and help us. The Christian journey is to be something uniquely different than our life-experience before coming to know Jesus Christ.

Unfortunately, many women get a rough start on this new path because they never learn what it means to enter into a relationship with Jesus. Instead, women often make a church or Christian people their new focus. There is only one sure-fire way to spiritual growth—connection to God through personal surrender to Jesus Christ.

bible study

Personal surrender is not a one-time event. Your new challenge is to open up your heart daily to Almighty God in fresh surrender. Being a follower of Christ is a lifelong process of denying our self while allowing Jesus Christ to come alive in us.

Read Luke 5:1-11 and Luke 9:23-25

What did Jesus ask Simon to do? What was Simon's reaction? What was the outcome of doing what Jesus had asked him to do?

Do you ever find yourself doubting God and questioning why he wants things done a certain way?

I think we all do. The passage in Luke 5 demonstrates an example of what happens when we let go of our own ways and obey God's voice. Simon went from catching nothing, to catching so many fish that the nets were breaking! Go figure! Do you suppose God knows when and where you are to go and what you are to do for purposeful living?

Why do you think Simon was afraid after catching all those fish? What did Simon and the other fishermen do when they realized the power of God working through Jesus?

Has there been a time in your life when you became aware of the awesome power of God? Explain how the acknowledgement of his power affected you? If you can't answer this personally, have you ever witnessed God working powerfully in another's life?

What do you think of the words, "they left everything and followed him"?

In Luke 9:23 what does Jesus say we must do to come to him?

What happens when we struggle to hold on to our own life?

Read Luke 9:57-62

The Bible is divided into the old and New Testament. The first four books of the New Testament are called the Gospels and contain eye witness accounts of Jesus' life on earth. Luke is one of the Gospels.

What did the first man say to Jesus?

This is a pretty broad statement. Interesting how Jesus brings a little reality into the cost of this man's promise!

What did the second and third man say to Jesus?

Do you ever find yourself in this same situation? *"I will follow you Jesus ... but first ..."*

To take up the cross is a picture of personal surrender and sacrifice. A disciple of Jesus is to give up her life to him. Many people use this phrase to refer to an illness, or negative experience. "This is just my cross to bear." But the statement of Jesus had more impact than just relinquishing to a negative experience.

In the times in which he spoke it, criminals carried their

cross after receiving a death sentence. Jesus calls us to take up our cross, burying our dreams, plans and agendas. As people dead to ourselves, he asks us to follow him. He will either resurrect our dreams or replace them with dreams and plans of his own. Though this is a hard concept, freedom comes when we lay down our lives. Note the use of the word "daily".

Follow me. Here we find the answer to connection! The word "follow" in the original language was used seventy-seven times in the gospels to mean: to accompany on a road, as part of a union. In our dictionary to follow means: to take as a guide, leader or example. There are many voices calling out to us in the world we live in. Which path will we follow? Jesus says that we are to follow him—and do it daily.

The new journey that we are on has many challenges. The biggest challenge is to remember how big God is, and how he is worthy of our lives and trust. It helps me to know that God cares deeply about me. When I am assured of this,

Deny yourself? This raises questions for most people. "Jesus was not talking about giving up sweets for Lent or denying oneself some small luxury. It is something far more radical: saying 'no' to the old self-centered way of living and thinking and saying 'yes' to Jesus." To deny yourself means that you are no longer the ruler and lord over your life—Jesus is. It is saying "no" to ourselves, our plans, our agendas—so that we can say yes to Him.

Norman Warren, *What's the Point*, Barbour Publishing, 31.

picking up my cross daily becomes a different thing entirely.

The following will help us begin to understand the heart of God toward us.

Read John 10:1-10

Note: If your Bible is a red-letter edition, the red (verses 1-5 and 7-10) represents the words of Christ.

What did Jesus call himself in verses 7 and 9?

Gate: an opening in a wall or fence, make access possible
Gatekeeper: one in charge of the gate
Shepherd: A man who tends a flock of sheep when they are at pasture. It is his job to guide and direct them; feed and protect them.

A shepherd is one who is very interested in the life and health of the flock. Jesus Christ is our shepherd, and he is interested in our emotional, spiritual, and physical life and health. This is real and this is practical.

In contrast to the Shepherd, what does the thief do (v. 10)?
  1.
  2.
  3.

What bold statement did Jesus make about his purpose, in relation to our lives (v.10)?

For some the thought of a full or abundant life means a

trouble-free existence. But that is not what Jesus is saying here. To have life to the full is to be complete in Christ, having all we need as a result of his power working in our lives. The advantage we have as believers is the power of God always at work in our midst.

Read John 10:17–30

What does the good shepherd do for the sheep?

What does it say the good shepherd's relationship is like with the sheep? (v. 14)

Know: The original Greek language here frequently indicates a relation between the person "knowing" and the object known. In this respect, what is known is of value or importance to the one who knows, and hence the establishment of relationship.

What three statements does verse 27 tell us?
1.
2.
3.

Often women hide from others and also from the God

who made them. We do this by wearing unseen masks or by staying busy with activities. We are great runners, and I am not talking about women in training for a marathon ... but rather, women who run the perfection and performance tracks, assuming that being better will be their ticket to approval or happiness. Listen to what the Bible says here, "I know my sheep ..."

I like to personalize Scripture. Personalizing makes it, "I know my Debbie ..." How does the personal application of that verse speak to your heart?

It is very evident here that Jesus intends for us to not only know him, but to follow him. It is also very evident that we can trust him, because he cares for us and nothing can take us out of his hand.

Psalm 100:3, 5

> *"Know that the Lord is God.*
> *It is he who made us, and we are his,*
> *we are his people, the sheep of his pasture.*
> *For the Lord is good and his love endures forever;*
> *his faithfulness continues through all generations."*

Nothing can take us out of his hand—we are his in an everlasting relationship. Relationships grow deeper as knowledge of one another grows. God already knows us perfectly. So the challenge is for us to learn to know him. But many things can hinder our growth in our relationship with him. To have power in our relationship we need to have a connection, and before that can happen we have to make a daily choice.

my plan

In every relationship, there are bound to be ups and downs. As you explore your new relationship with Christ, there will be times when you feel incredibly close to him—and other times when he may seem distant. In those "distant" times, remember that he's not the one who moved! I like to use three simple R's as a check system in my walk with Christ:

Remain- How do we remain in him? In John 15:10, Jesus says, "If you obey my commands, you will remain in my love ..." This is a key to living each day in a personal relationship with the Father. Remaining is staying connected by reading and obeying his word.

Renew- Each day is a fresh start with Jesus. When you are connected to God through his Word and prayer, the Holy Spirit flows in you and your heart and mind are renewed. "Do not conform any longer to the pattern of this world, but be transformed by the renewing of your mind. Then you will be able to test and approve what God's will is—his good, pleasing and perfect will." Romans 12:2

Rest- We can be women who have peace, and there is rest for us! Philippians 4:6-7 tells us that the way to peace is to take everything to God in prayer and thanksgiving. God's peace transcends our understanding and guards our hearts when our minds are on Him.

Remain,
Renew,
Rest!

Remember that childhood game, follow the leader? That is exactly what we are to do on this new journey with God.

We look into his Word to see where he is going, what he values, what he is all about. We talk to him in prayer. We connect to him daily.

Are you connected? Remember, to be connected is to be hooked up, interlinked, dependent. Ask yourself these three questions to measure your connectedness in your relationship with Christ:

* *Have I plugged in to Christ today?*
* *Have I allowed his Word to speak to me today?*
* *Have I made the choice to turn over to God everything that happens today?*

Connecting with God begins when we put aside our wants and choose to follow Christ. This is a daily choice. The nearer we are to Christ, the easier it is to stay connected. God has promised that as we come near to him, he will close the gap and come near to us (James 4:8). As we set our hearts to follow the leader, we take the first steps of a new journey for a new life!

Dear God,
I want to be connected to you. Teach me how—make each new day a fresh start. I thank you for being my shepherd, for loving me and calling me by name. May I learn to trust you because you care for me. Help me to put the past behind me. Enable me to stay connected with you today, tomorrow, and every day of this new journey.

In Jesus' Name—Amen

connecting:

our new relationship with others

G od is love. We want to grow to be more like him, but we have a lifelong challenge—getting along with people! Sometimes we don't want to hear that we are called to love other people. Sure, it's easy to love those who love us. But what about those who rub us the wrong way, think differently than us, have different personalities—or worse yet, purposefully hurt us?

Maybe you have seen this "Daily Prayer":

> *So far today, God,*
> *I've done all right ...*
> *I haven't gossiped.*
> *I haven't been grumpy, nasty or selfish.*
> *I'm really glad of that,*
> *But in a few minutes, God,*
> *I'm going to get out of bed,*
> *From now on, I'm probably going to*
> *Need a lot of help.*

It would be easy to love others if I were living alone on a mountaintop or tucked away in a private cave. There in the quietness and peace of not having to deal with other people, I could think about God's love and come up with some great theory. In this place, I could love everybody and everything. There would be nothing to stop me from love—no disappointments, no disagreements, and no conflict.

But none of us live in a cave or on a mountaintop. Instead we are living in homes with people who rub us the wrong way, say the wrong things, and often take us for granted. We are working in offices with people of different interests, different backgrounds, and different personalities. Add to the mix all the complex relationships of today—in-laws, out-laws, and ex-laws—and you have a real challenge.

> *"'Love the Lord your God with all your heart and with all your soul and with all your mind and with all your strength.' The second is this: 'Love your neighbor as yourself.' There is no commandment greater than these." Mark 12:30-31*

- *Relationship to God*
- *Relationship with others*

When we come to Jesus Christ and begin following him, there is not an automatic switch that is flipped on called the love switch. Too bad. If there were, there would be no need for this commandment or for scriptural instruction. As we look at God's Word together, we will begin building a relationship style that is built on a good and solid foundation—God's love.

bible study

Read John 17

As you read, keep in mind that this is Jesus praying. Pay close attention to what he is saying to the Father about you. Often our lack of love for others is an indication of our insecurity. Here we see the reason for security and peace. We also see that God gives us the necessary key to living a life of love because God is love.

Write out John 17:15-17

In John 17, I find hope in the following truths:
- *Jesus has authority over me (v. 2)*
- *Jesus gives me eternal life (v. 3)*
- *I am his (v. 10)*
- *I am protected (v. 12)*
- *I am given joy (v. 13)*
- *I have his word (v. 14)*

Remember that his word teaches and instructs us, and is good for showing us what will work for us in life and what won't. Sanctify means to set apart. Here Jesus is asking the Father to keep us set apart by the Word of God, which is the truth. He also tells us that the truth of his Word will set us free (John 8:32).

We can see that it is the heart of Jesus and the plan of God that we would be set apart and set free. Unlocked from the unhealthy patterns of this world, we become free to now love God's way. We become free to have a relationship with God, the maker of all things. And, free to have healthy relationships with those whom he has made.

Write out John 17:26

God Himself in me? Wow! Now that is powerful! Could it be that God could express his love through me to others? Once we get it firmly established in our minds that God Himself lives in us and wants to work through us, life becomes different.

Read the following verses, each having to do with the word impossible. Do you find it impossible to love others sometimes?
- *Luke 1:37*
- *Luke 18:27*
- *Matthew 17:20*
- *Hebrews 11:6*

Write out Romans 5:5

It is not impossible for us to love because we have the source of love living inside of us. In 1 Corinthians 13 we see the characteristics of God's love toward us, and we can also see God's pattern of loving others with that same love. These attributes of God's love are the very traits that he can work into our hearts and lives as we abide in Him. His love is our pattern.

Make a list of the qualities or the patterns of love you have seen demonstrated by Christ to you. For example, forgiving.

Do these qualities also characterize you in your relationship with others?

Read 2 Timothy 2:22

According to this verse, what are the four things you are to pursue?

    1.

    2.

    3.

    4.

Pursue: To run or chase after. In this definition I see that a directional choice is the first step. We have explored the importance of choice. Our daily choices to draw near to God, to confess our sins to God, and to follow God are the foundation for this new life. In addition, we have a daily choice to pursue or chase after love and peace!

Read 1 John 2:9-14, 1 John 3:11-16, 1 John 4:7-9

When we live within the parameters of hate, what are we also living in?

What happens when we begin walking in love?

What does darkness do to us?

Why did Cain hate his brother?

Do you think jealousy or insecurity causes relationship problems?

Where does love come from?

Why did God send his Son into the world? (1 John 4:9)
Write out 1 John 4:9

The emphasis here is: live through him. Nothing is impossible when living through God's power and Spirit. It's when we are living within the smallness of our own love, feelings, insecurities and fears that we have trouble.

Let's look at some practical scriptural directives in our relationships with others.

Read Ephesians 4:25-32
According to these verses what grieves the Holy Spirit?

What are you to get rid of?

How are you to live?

What happens when anger spills over day after day?

Does this passage suggest that you are never to be angry?

Verse 31 tells us to get rid of some things. What are they?

Verse 32 tells us three keys to good relationships. What are they?

Read Psalm 4:4-5

These verses give us direction for our anger. Write how you could apply this.

Being a Christian does not eliminate all human emotion. We still get hurt, angry, disappointed and sad. But as we

The salvation that comes through Christ may be described in three tenses: past, present, and future. When a person believes in Christ, she is saved (Acts 16:31). But we are also in the process of being saved from the power of sin (Romans 8:13; Philippians 2:12). Finally, we shall be saved from the very presence of sin (Romans 13:11; Titus 2:12-13). God releases into our lives today the power of Christ's resurrection (Romans 6:4) and allows us a foretaste of our future life as His children (2 Corinthians 1:22; Ephesians 1:14). Our experience of salvation will be complete when Christ returns (Hebrews 9:28) and the kingdom of God is fully revealed (Matthews 13:41-43).

The Liberty Illustrated Bible Dictionary, Thomas Nelson Publishers, 1968, 939.

read God's Word, we see healthy directives for living. As we look to the Word of God for answers, the Holy Spirit leads us and guides us into all truth.

Read Matthew 5:38-48

Is the relational instruction of Jesus a popular way to live? (vv. 38-42)

What are we to do with our enemies? (v. 44)

Are we to love only those deserving of our love?

Write out Luke 6:38

This would be a good verse to take to heart in all of your relationships. These are the words of Christ, and so we would be wise to take them as serious truth!

Once we have come to Christ our relationships have new possibility. No longer do we rely just on our own love, but now on God's love that has been placed in our hearts. Our relationships should be different because we are different.

my plan

Our relationships should be a reflection of who we are becoming, who we are living for, and whose power we are trusting in. When relying on the love of Christ, we will be loving, patient and kind people. When our focus is on ourselves, we will be irritable, easily angered, unforgiving and pitiful people.

The focus is the key. We live in a world that focuses on "self" Everything is all about "me." But to walk in this new life, we must pray for the grace to go from "me-living" to "he-living." When this begins to happen, everything within us and around us begins to settle down and change.

The following list reflects God's way of relating to others. Prayerfully review the characteristics, thinking about how each is reflected in your relationships to others, and circle three that you would like to focus on this week:

God's Most Excellent Way—A Pattern of Love
- *Patient*
- *Does Not Envy*
- *Not Proud*
- *Not Self-Seeking*
- *Forgiving*
- *Trusting*
- *Persevering*
- *Kind*
- *Does Not Boast*
- *Not Rude*
- *Not Easily Angered*
- *Protecting*
- *Hopeful*

Each of us must deal with obstacles within our own human flesh and within imperfect relationships. Prayerfully circle the obstacles you are willing to have God deal with in you this week so that you may walk in God's pattern, the most excellent way:

Our Self-Focused Way—Obstacles to Love

- *Defensiveness*
- *Pride*
- *Stubbornness*
- *Bitter*
- *Judgmental*
- *Jealous*
- *Selfish*
- *Payback*
- *Anger*
- *Neediness*
- *Unforgiving*
- *Hateful*
- *Critical*
- *Competitive*
- *Insecure*
- *Rude*

Dear God,

I am imperfect and so are my relationships with others. I ask you to fill me with your love, that I might be a conduit of love to those who are in my life. Take away the obstacles to love within me and teach me your perfect pattern for loving others. *In Jesus' Name—Amen*

connecting

to God, our Father

James and Madison always wanted children. Year after year they hoped to conceive until they discovered they would not be able to have a child of their own. At times my friends longing for a baby was agonizing to watch. Eventually, they decided to go through the long, tedious process of adoption. But because they wanted this child so much, the process was never too tedious nor too difficult.

After many prayers, hopes, and tears, the adoption process was finally complete. God gave them the desire of their heart—Amy Michele. She was now the object of their every desire and attention. The heartbeat of their day was spent meeting her needs. The joy of their life was to raise this precious little girl.

Do James and Madison love Amy as much as they would love a birth child? You bet they do—maybe even more—because of their persistent pursuit of her. They understand and appreciate the cost of bringing this child into their family.

We have a God who understands about adoption. Our God so desperately wanted you and me to be a part of his family, he submitted to a very difficult and costly adoption process. He sent Jesus to pay the price of bringing us into the family of God. Jesus endured suffering and ultimately death. The cost he paid and the pain he bore brought all who would believe in him into the adoption process, making us God's children.

For some, its a stretch to think of God as a parent and us as his children. But in reality, we are not merely the product of two lovestruck people we learned to call parents. Nor are we the result of a mistake or an accident by two people who maybe didn't welcome our arrival into the world.

Regardless of how you got your earthly start, your life is a miracle of God's design. It started with your birth and now will continue through your spiritual rebirth. You are God's precious daughter who has now been born again in the spiritual sense.

> *"Flesh gives birth to flesh, but the Spirit gives birth to spirit. You should not be surprised at my saying, 'You must be born again.'"* John 3:6

Those two words, born again, are beautiful. Without the Spirit of the living God giving birth to our spirit, we would be forever dead, dull, and without life. But because of the love of God toward us, though we were born in the flesh, we now can live in the power of our Heavenly Father!

bible study

A good father-child relationship comes with unique benefits: a name, a family, love and security, and an inheritance. As you study what Scripture says about relating to God as your Father, remember these benefits as they apply to God's children.

Read John 1:10-13

Who is the "He" in this passage?

What right is given to those who believe in Jesus?

Read 1 John 3:1-2; 4:9-16

This "new name" given to us is a direct result of something wonderful that has been lavished on us—what does Scripture say that is?

How did God demonstrate love to us?

As one who believes in Christ, you have been given a new name—child of God—with all the rights and responsibilities that go with being part of God's family.

Write out 1 John 4:16:

According to this verse, what are the two things we are to do?
  1.
  2.

I don't think we have much trouble knowing about God's love in our head. But relying on it is where we get stuck. Relying takes the reality of his love from head to heart and impacts our life in "real" ways. In order to live as a child of God, you will need to learn to rely on his love for you. His love is the signature on your new adoption papers! Your worth is based on the signature of God on your life!

Read Romans 8:15-17
What Spirit did you receive?

What can you now call God?

Abba is the Aramaic for Father. We have been adopted as his children. Children he wanted and loved. We can now call him, "Daddy, Daddy." For some this is hard to take due to painful memories in unhealthy father relationships here on earth. But through Jesus we can experience healing of the pain in our past.

Remember, he came to bind up the brokenhearted! He has been with each of us through every pain, every tear, and every misunderstanding. Your heavenly Father cares. We are now His children.

If we are his children, what does it also say we are?

Heir: A person who inherits rank or property from the owner of such. The legal heir, especially in relation to a throne, whose claim cannot be set aside.

Write out 2 Corinthians 6:18

This is not a relationship based on a "maybe" or contingent on an "if." This is God's promise to you. If we will embrace this truth, we will have peace. As his children, we can rest in the truth that he loves us and always has our best interest in mind. He is our Father, the one and only, who has marked us as his.

Read Ephesians 2:1-10

When we were not living in Christ, how were we living? What were we satisfying?

Is salvation something we just chose? Is our choice something to boast about?

What does verse 8 call salvation?

What does verse 10 call us? What is our purpose?

Workmanship here is the original Greek word that means: poem or work of art. You are God's masterpiece, his poetry, his painting. He has prepared good things for your life: fruitfulness, blessing, honor. He will now give you the power and strength to walk in what he has prepared for you since the beginning of time.

Read Matthew 6:25-33

If something in the Bible is unclear to you, pray and ask the Master Teacher—the Holy Spirit—to help you understand it. In these passages concentrate on what it means for Jesus to be your Father.

The everlasting power and Divinity of God is revealed in creation. However, the Fatherhood of God is possible only through a spiritual relationship brought about through our adoption as children of God. It is a relationship established through faith in the Son, Jesus Christ. As the only begotten Son, Jesus alone can call God Father apart from the work of grace. The revelation of God as Father is the subject of the New Testament and waited for the presence on earth of the Son, Matthew 11:27; John 17:25. Whereas all humanity can relate to God as the Creator, only those who have been adopted into God's family can enter into a relationship with God as Father.

W. E. Vine, *An Expository Dictionary of New Testament Words*, Fleming H. Revell Company, 1966, Vol. 2, 81-82.

In this passage, we are instructed what "not" to do. What are we instructed "not" to do?

We are not to worry because of our relationship to our heavenly Father. What are we told about God in these verses?

Matthew tells us that our heavenly Father values us (v. 26), knows what we need (v. 32), and will give you what you need. That kind of trust in the Father's provision is not the way of the world. In fact, verse 32 tells us that the pagans run after all these things.

What is a pagan? I don't like the way it even sounds, but I should know what it means if I am to learn what not to be ... don't you think?

Pagan: A follower of a false god or a heathen religion. One who delights in material things. An unbeliever.

Wow! Here is a perfect example of how we are to live differently. If we KNOW that our heavenly Father values us and is taking care of us, then we will not run after things, worry about things, be filled with anxiety. Why? Because that is what a loving father does! And our heavenly Father does it perfectly.

Growing up I memorized The Lord's Prayer (Matthew 6:9-13), the "Our Father" as we called it. I knew the words, but unfortunately the meaning never penetrated my heart. Today as I read this Scripture prayer, I see an attitude of complete surrender and trust in my Father.

Do you feel comfortable going to God, as a father who cares for you? Why or why not?

Even in the worst of times, most parents will bend their heart to a need of their child. Luke 11:13 tells us that even human parents, with a natural bent toward evil, know how to give good gifts to our children. We give according to our means and out of abundant love. But even the most loving, giving, caring, earthly parent cannot outgive God.

Read Galatians 4:4-7

Becoming a child of God has certain rights and privileges—and responsibilities. God's ways are perfect. In his perfect time, God sent his only "birth" son, Jesus, to secure for us all the rights and privileges he himself enjoys with the Father.

Because we are God's child, what does he send into our hearts? What is the result?

Remember, "Abba, Father" is a term of endearment. It means we can call the creator of the universe "Daddy."

What were we before we became God's childen?

God's Word tells us that until we accept Jesus as Savior and enter into our new relationship with God as Father, we are slaves to sin, slaves to the law, and slaves to our old nature (Gal. 3:22-23; Rom. 7:25).

What does verse 7 say we are now?

Now that God is your Father, you have access to God through the Spirit living in you. You are no longer a slave but an heir to a heavenly kingdom—one that will never decay or be destroyed—where you will live forever in the light of your Father's love.

Read 1 John 4:16-18

God is love. This is the very nature of who and what God is all about. Too often God gets the bad rap for the wrong choices made by people, or for the bad things that happen to us throughout the course of life. But it isn't God who is the author of evil. He is a God of love.

We live in an imperfect world. Still, according to verse 16, what can we rely on?

What does the perfect love of God drive out?

God desires to keep us from the evil of this imperfect world—by his love, protection, and grace. As you learn more about the perfect love of your Father God, you will be able to live without fear even in the midst of an evil world.

Cut 1
line

my plan

Want to see a picture of your Father? Read 1 Corinthians 13. These are the attributes of love, and since God is love, this is the face and character of God our Father:

- *Love is patient*
- *Love is kind*
- *Love does not envy*
- *Love does not boast*
- *Love is not proud*
- *Love is not rude*
- *Love is not self-seeking*
- *Love is not easily angered*
- *Love keeps no records of wrongs*
- *Love does not delight in evil*
- *Love rejoices in the truth*
- *Love always protects*
- *Love always trusts*
- *Love always hopes*
- *Love always perseveres*
- *Love never fails.*

This is your Father. This is how he relates to you. Choose one attribute of love listed here and record how you have seen God demonstrate it in your life:

Your Father is the King—filled with love and compassion, patience and gentleness. As we grow in this knowledge, it will help us discover who we are, and we will know the meaning of living like princesses. Not like little spoiled-princesses, but princesses who follow in the love of their Father's steps!

Your Father wants you to show his love to others as a demonstration of your new relationship with him. Choose an attribute of love from 1 Corinthians 13 and make a plan on how you will demonstrate that attribute to someone this week:

Dear God,

Now I see that I can call you Father! What a privilege to have such a personal relationship with you. I thank you for paying the price so I could be adopted as your own child. Let me grow in the knowledge of what it means to be in you, live through you, and be your daughter. You are the King of Kings, and I am your princess. Lead me and guide me to walk in a way that would please you and give you honor.

In Jesus' Name—Amen

connecting

to our families

How many times have you blown it? Do you ever feel like God is going to give up on you? Sometimes I have felt that way. And based on how irritable or impatient I can get with others, it's no wonder I have often come to the conclusion that God is irritable and impatient with me too. But the truth is—he is not like us.

Sheila is a woman who has been allowing me to walk with her through some very difficult times. She has made grave mistakes, but she desires now to seek God and his plan for her life. The problem with Sheila is not her mistakes—those are her past. The problem with Sheila is her inability, or unwillingness, to let go of those mistakes and receive God's forgiveness—trusting him with a new future.

Forgiveness is often most difficult in family relationships. Unlike other relationships that you can move away from or avoid, your family is with you for life! As you move into a new relationship with Christ, your relationships with your parents, your siblings, your spouse, your children, and your extended family will begin to take on a new dynamic that will stretch your faith in new ways. Forgiveness will be key as you seek to connect to your families.

From the beginning, God saw the need for family. Family relationships were meant to be a blessing to us but sin messed that up. Even Adam and Eve experienced trouble in familyland. Try to imagine the first conversation between husband and wife after being sent out of Paradise! Do you think Eve was over-protective of Seth after she lost two sons—one murdered and the other cast out?

Let's face it! Sometimes the family ties can feel more like shackles. Some of us, like Sheila, get stuck in the past. That can happen easily with family members since your past is so intricately tied to them. But God encourages us live a better way:

> *Forget the former things;*
> *do not dwell on the past.*
> *See, I am doing a new thing!*
> *Isaiah 43:18*

In this lesson we will look at the amazing forgiveness of God, and the blessing we can live in as the child who is corrected and shaped by an all wise, all loving, all knowing Father. We will see how, regardless of our family past, we can live with our families in a healthy, godly way.

We will also look at some guidelines God has given us in his Word for living lovingly as daughters, wives, mothers, sisters, and even daughter-in-laws. God wants us to connect to our families and his Word can show us how.

bible study

Read Psalm 51:3-4

Though we try to cover it up, what do we know?

When we fall short, who are we accountable to?

The first and most important step toward forgiveness is owning up to what we are and what we have done. This is called confession. When we blow it, we must own it—and we confess what we have done that is wrong before God. confession should lead to repentence—a desire to change our behavior.

Read Psalm 51:7-9

What is happening in this verse?

What is being asked for?

Read 1 John 1:8-10

What happens to us when we claim to be without fault or sin?

What happens if we admit we have failed?

What are the two things that happen when we confess our sin to God?

What two words describe the nature of God toward us as we confess?

Read Hebrews 8:12; Psalm 103:12; Isaiah 38:17
What happens when God forgives our sin?

How often does God take out our sin and look at it?

When God forgives, he forgets—not because he is forgetful but because he is loving. He does not want our sin to interfere with our relationship to him. He is our model of how to forgive and let go of the past so that our relationships with those we love can thrive.

All of Scripture is about relationships.

- *Our relationship with God*
- *Our relationship with self*
- *Our relationship with others*

Relationships are the very thing that makes up life. God has been interested in relationships since the beginning of time. He and he alone has the answers, and the wisdom to navigate us through a lifetime of relationships. his word can give use principles to live by in our relationships with our family.

Read Ephesians 5:22-24

Nowhere is the daily walk of a Christian put more to the test than in the most intimate of relationships—the marriage relationship.

What are wives called to do as to the Lord?

What does submission mean to you?

What model of submission has God given us?

Paul wrote this passage to believers. So, what if your husband is not a believer?

Read 1 Peter 3:1

Why should wives or unbelieving husbands submit?

What two characteristics are to be visible in your life?

Still feeling uneasy about submitting? 1 Peter 3:1 starts out "In the same way ..." What way? If you look at the previous chapter, it becomes evident that submission in this case is

Submission is a difficult concept to our modern minds. It conjures up visions of servitude and degradation. But that is not how God envisions submission. It takes a study of the whole of God's word to understand that submission is both admirable and desirable because it is both mutual and God-pleasing. Submission within the marriage relationship demonstrates the deep love and respect with which Christ approaches his relationship to the church. "This passage is an expression of God's ideal for marriage. The marriage relationship was designed by him to be symbolic of the spiritual relationship between Christ and the Church... The obligations are not merely one-sided. The husband's responsibility is just as binding as that of the wife. "

The Wycliffe Bible Commentary, Moody Press, 1962, 1314.

not an indication that one person is better than another but that submission is necessary to bring order to the home.

Christ, again, is our example. He willingly submitted to the will of his Father. If he had not, where would our salvation be?

Read Deuteronomy 5:16 to discover the first commandment with a promise attached

In this commandment from the Ten Commandments, what are we told to do? What is the promise?

How do we honor our fathers and mothers?

Honor means to esteem or value as precious. It is our duty to honor our parents in word and deed regardless of whether or not we think they have "earned" or "deserve"' it.

The true nature of our commitment and love to our families often reveals itself most clearly during times of adversity.

Read Ruth 1:3-9

The book of Ruth was written during just such a time. There is a famine in the land. Ruth's husband, father-in-law, and brother-in-law are all dead. She has no one left to provide for her—to redeem her from physical peril and social disgrace.

What was Ruth's relationship to Naomi?

What was Naomi planning to do?

What was Naomi's advice to her daughters-in-law, Ruth and Orpah?

Read Ruth 1:10–18

How would you describe Naomi's emotional state?

What was Orpah's decision?

How does Ruth respond to Naomi's continued urging that she leave her?

The words in Ruth 1:16 are often recited during wedding ceremonies as a pledge of love and loyalty between a husband and wife. But in the context, this pledge is between two women related through marriage.

Ruth's connectedness to her mother-in-law is a wonderful model of how we can be in relationship with our mothers and other mother-figures in our lives. And, by the way, Ruth is an ancestor to King David and Jesus.

Read John 1:40–21

Who was Andrew?

What was the first thing Andrew did after he found Jesus?

The first thing Andrew did was bring his brother, Simon Peter, to Christ. Do you have a brother or sister who needs to be brought to Jesus? What can you do to help bring them to Christ?

Read Matthew 18:21-22

What question does Peter ask Jesus?

How does Jesus answer him?

Simon Peter asks Jesus "How many times do I have to forgive my brother?" Can you hear the whine in his voice? "But Lord! It's his fault! *He* sinned against *me*!" I wonder if this is the same brother, Andrew, who brought Peter to Christ in the first place!

In his answer, and in the story that follows (Matthew 18:23-35) Jesus makes it clear that forgiving our brothers (and sisters) is our responsibility. And we are to keep on forgiving in proportion to how much God has forgiven us. Do you see now why it is important for you to understand the depth of God's forgiveness toward you?

my plan

We all make mistakes and we all sin. But Christ has made a way for us to experience God's forgiveness.

List three things you know to be true about God's forgiveness:

1.

2.

3.

As you experience God's forgiveness, it is important to put the past behind you and move confidently into the new future God has planned. Is there anything from your past that you need to give to God right now?

Your new relationship with God will enable you to have healthier relationships with your family. What one family relationship do you feel God is asking you to focus on this week?

Write a prayer to God asking for his wisdom in how he

wants you to relate to this person this week. As you pray, focus on three things:

1. *Confess any behavior or feelings you feel are not honoring God in this relationship and ask God to forgive you:*

2. *Ask God to reveal to you specifically how your actions toward this person should change:*

3. *Thank God for revealing to you his truths about family relationships and for giving you the strength to live love and honor with your family.*

Dear God,

I thank you that I can come to you, even with the smallest thing—and ask you to forgive me. I thank you that my connection with you each day can equip me to live with my family as I should. Make me all that you've intended me to be. I want to walk with you every day.

In Jesus' Name—Amen

connecting

to the Holy Spirit

In order for us to be fully equipped for godly relationships with others, we must understand the relationship within The Trinity—or what some call the Three-Person God. Scripture teaches that God is one, yet three distinct Persons: Father, Son, and Holy Spirit. Each is independent, but never acts independently. Each is a distinct person, but they are one in purpose, in essence and in nature. In our minds this is hard to comprehend, so we must accept it by faith.

Most often as we grow in Christ, we study the life and character of Jesus. We understand that even though he is the Son, he is also God. Things can get a little confusing as we seek to understand the Spirit of God, and the Trinity. We have studied our relationship to God the Father. The Holy Spirit is also fully divine and has personal qualities, yet with a distinct role separate from the Father and Son.

There is no verse in the Bible that uses the word Trinity. The idea of the Trinity came about because of biblical teaching that equated the Son and the Holy Spirit with God and because of our experience of God. The following is a description of the Trinity by C.S. Lewis:

"People already knew about God in a vague way. Then came a man who claimed to be God; and yet He was not the sort of man you could dismiss as a lunatic. He made them believe Him. They met Him again after they had seen Him killed. And then, after they had been formed into a little society or community, they found God somehow inside them as well; directing them, making them able to do things they could not do before. And when they have worked it out they found they had arrived at the Christian definition of the three-personal God."

With the promise of his Spirit comes the promise of power. This power is not for personal abuse or selfish use. Instead, this power has been graciously provided by the Father to equip us and lead us through life. The power of the Holy Spirit makes personal growth possible.

Personal growth is big business these days. There are seminars, classes, books, and programs on almost every subject relating to personal or spiritual growth. Sometimes it seems like we, as a people, are huffing and puffing our way through life. Unfortunately, our desire to grow will only be just that—huffing and puffing—until we realize the power of God's Spirit alive within us.

In this lesson we will look at the Trinity, and discover how the Holy Spirit was given to us, in order that we might walk in the life of God, the essence of God himself.

bible study

Read Deuteronomy 6:1-9

Write out Deuteronomy 6:4

Why do you think it is important to emphasize that there is one God?

Read 2 Corinthians 13:14

Do you see the three persons of God in this verse?

What characteristic is associated with each member of the Trinity?

What does this tell us about their individual roles?

The Trinity

God exists as three persons (referred to as the Trinity)—yet he is one.

- *The Father is God invisible—John 1:18*
- *The Son is God revealed—John 1:14-18, Hebrews 1:1-4*
- *The Holy Spirit is God working in men—John 16:8, 1 Corinthians 2:10-11 and 6:19-20. (Other*

passages that teach about the Trinity are: Matthew 3:16-17 and 28:19; John 14:16; 2 Corinthians 13:14; and 1 Peter 1:2)

Read Acts 5:1-4

How do these verses demonstrate that the Holy Spirit is God?

Do you see how the Holy Spirit is a personal and divine source?

When Ananias and Sapphira forfeited their lives, to whom had they lied?

The Bible explains what kind of relationship we can have with the Holy Spirit. Let's ask the important question, *Who is the Holy Spirit?*

Read the following verses, and note the activity or characteristic of the Holy Spirit.

- *Ephesians 4:30*
- *Acts 13:2*
- *1 Corinthians 2:10*
- *1 Corinthians 2:12-13*
- *1 Corinthians 12:11*

Do you think these verses indicate that the Holy Spirit is a real person, though not a physical one? Explain what you see here in Scripture.

In the Bible, the Holy Spirit has several names, including: Comforter, Spirit of Truth, Spirit of Christ, Spirit of Jesus, and Spirit of God.

Read the following verses, and note how they indicate that the Holy Spirit is God.
- *Genesis 1:2*

- *Hebrews 9:14*

- *Psalm 139:7-8*

Read John 3:5-6 , Ephesians 1:13-14 and Titus 3:5
How is the Holy Spirit involved at the time of salvation?

What deposit has been placed within you?

What word is used in the Titus verse to describe the work of the Holy Spirit in us?

Read Romans 8:9-17
Do you see evidence here that the Spirit of God lives within you?

What is our new obligation?

Is there indication that the Holy Spirit imparts freedom?

Read 1 Corinthians 3:16, and 12:13
What are you described as?

What has happened to every member of the body of Christ?

Read John 16:7-15
How is the Holy Spirit working today? (vv. 8-11)

What is he doing for believers? (v. 13)

What is his emphasis to us? (vv. 14-15)

Read John 15:1-17
What does Jesus call himself here?

How does he describe the Father here? What is his work?

Write out John 15:4

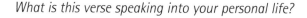

What is this verse speaking into your personal life?

What cannot happen apart from connection with Jesus?

What brings glory to the Father? (vv. 7-8)

What has God appointed us to do? (v. 16)

God has appointed us to bear fruit, but we must remember that this will not happen apart from him. It is only as we are connected to Jesus that his power can flow through us. I often liken it to plugging into a power outlet. The current or energy running through us when we are plugged in to Jesus—is the Holy Spirit of God!

> *"To this end I labor, struggling with all his energy, which so powerfully works in me."*
> *Colossians 1:29*

Read the following verses:
- **Acts 2:38**

    What is the gift you have received?

Gift: A thing given or received without payment
- **Acts 1:8**

    What will you receive when the Holy Spirit comes on you?

    What will you be equipped for?

Read the following verses to understand the Holy Spirit:
- **John 4:24—God is a Spirit**

Power in the original language is *dunamis* which means: ability, might, to be made able.

Here is a lawn mower analogy to help you remember how this works: Gas makes the lawn mower function, and without the gas there is not the ability to get the job done. Gas gives the lawn mower might and ability. Gas makes the lawn mower able for the task. Likewise, we need the power of the Holy Spirit to equip us and make us able for everything God has set before us. No longer are we unable. Now we have God's Spirit. Apart from connection we are still dysfunctional and unable. But, connected to God, and the power of his Spirit, under the authority of Jesus—we are able for everything and anything God places before us!

How are we to worship God?

Does this differ from serving him with perfection and rules?

- **2 Peter 1:21—He authored the Scriptures**
  How does this verse shed new light on the Word of God?

- **John 16:13—He guides into all truth**
  Do you ever feel you need someone to light your way?

  What does this verse say the Holy Spirit will be for you?

- **John 14:26—The Father has sent him into the world**
  What is another name for the Holy Spirit in this verse?

  What will he do for you?

- **John 14:17—He dwells within believers**
  Where is the Holy Spirit right now?

- **Romans 8:16—He confirms that we are God's own**
  If you have trouble believing that you are a new person upon salvation, whom can you ask to make that clear and real to your heart?

my plan

There is one God and only one God. Yet he exists in three different persons and we can have a relationship with each one. This is a mystery! Yet it is so clearly revealed to be true in Scripture, we can accept it by faith. These are the three workings of the same God.

- *God the Father—the invisible God, who created all things*
- *God the Son—the visible God, who came in human form to redeem mankind*
- *God the Spirit—the essence of God at work within each believer's life*

We came into the world as spiritual orphans, and God adopted us into his eternal family. He draws us into his life, for that is the very reason we exist—for relationship with the Father, Son, and Holy Spirit.

It is clear in Scripture that it is the Holy Spirit in us who brings us into the family of God. We are adopted into the life that is shared between the Father and the Son. Being a Christian means receiving adoption papers! It is the very life of the Holy Spirit within us that causes us to cry, "Abba Father!"

What does it mean to you to be adopted into the family of Father, Son, and Holy Spirit?

One of the benefits of our adoption is that we can tap into the power of the Holy Spirit to live the life God has called us to live. But we have the responsibility to discover and use this power.

In his book, *The Search for Freedom*, Robert McGee tells a story that best illustrates the point of untapped power.

"If I wanted to mow my yard, I could go to the garage, take out my mower, and start pushing it in circles around my lawn. But would that get the job done? It depends. As long as the mower was working properly, my efforts would not be in vain. But what if it didn't have any gas in it? What if the spark plug wire was disconnected? What if I neglected to start it before I started mowing? Any of these problems could prevent me from doing what I had set out to do. Not only would I be working hard with no result, I would also look silly to observers. And when I finally realized what I was doing, I might feel foolish as well."

Each day we have a choice to make. Will we approach life with or without the power of the Holy Spirit? How can you tap into the power of the Holy Spirit today?

Dear God,

Thank you for showing me yourself through your word. There are so many mysteries, so much to grasp. Your Holy Spirit will teach me, and I thank you that your Spirit was placed within me when I received you. May I receive daily the work of your Spirit within my life.

In Jesus' Name—Amen

connecting
to other believers

The sign out front said "Open House" so Elizabeth went in to take a look around. She had always admired these particular townhouses—they seemed like individual little bungalows just slightly connected together. The wooded areas around each grouping of homes lent an air of solitude and tranquility.

The inside of a stranger's home can be very revealing. Elizabeth wandered through the downstairs rooms, peeking into closets and cupboards at the invitation of the owner. On the stairway wall leading to the master suite upstairs, Elizabeth paused to admire several pictures of elementary age children and a plaque with a Scripture verse.

Thinking that she had found a fellow-believer in this single mother, Elizabeth asked the townhouse owner what church she attended.

"Oh, I don't go to church," the attractive blond woman replied. "I have a relationship with God but I have no use for the church," she concluded.

Stunned, Elizabeth said no more. She concluded her tour of the home and thanked the owner for showing her around.

It wasn't until she was driving away in her car that Elizabeth realized how much the woman's words had grieved her.

God has called us to be in relationship with other believers. Believers are intricately connected, as different parts of one body. In your new relationship with Christ, it is important that you connect to a body of believers that will encourage you to grow.

Every believer has a responsibility to other believers—whether they are a part of your church family or not. This isn't an easy relationship because there is a lot of diversity in the body of Christ. There are many churches and many denominations—all with their own particular way of doing things like worship, missions, giving, etc. This can be especially confusing to those who are just beginning their walk with Christ.

But God has called us to unity. Before he left this earth, Jesus prayed to his Father in heaven for all his followers. He prayed:

> *"May they be brought to complete unity to let the world know that you sent me and have loved them even as you have loved me" John 17:23.*

In this study, we will look at Jesus' prayer in more detail. We will also look at the work of the Holy Spirit in empowering us to live as part of the body of Christ and how we are to act toward other believers in Christ.

bible study

Read John 17

This is a prayer of Jesus Christ. He is making truth statements about our position in Christ, and praying for us—his people.

Who does Jesus have authority over (v. 2)?

What is the result of knowing Jesus (v. 3)?

Who is Jesus praying for (v. 9)?

What does Jesus ask the Father to do so that we may be one (v. 11)?

Jesus recognized that without his presence with the early believers, it would difficult for them to stay together. He prayed that his followers would be as united in love as he and the Father are. But he also knew it would be an area in which Satan would attack (v. 15).

In John 17:20, who does Jesus say he is praying for?

Jesus' prayer for believers was not just for his disciples or the early church. It was for us! Imagine! He is preparing to face his death on the cross and he took time to pray that there would a oneness of spirit—for you and me and all believers. Sounds important, doesn't it?

Read Acts 2:44-47

What do you see that indicates Jesus' prayer was answered in the early church?

What was the result of the believer's love for each other (v. 47)?

What do you think happened between John 17 and Acts 2 that made this kind of relationship among the believers possible?

Jesus was looking ahead to the coming of the Holy Spirit into the lives of all believers. It is the Holy Spirit that empowers us to live as we should with our fellow brothers and sisters in Christ.

Read Galatians 5:16-21

What power are you told to live by?

I like to personalize things. In my Bible , I have jotted my name in this verse, so it now reads:

So I say, Debbie, live by the Spirit and you will not gratify the desires of your sinful nature.

Somehow the personalization helps me realize that it is not an abstract, but rather a very personal directive for my everyday life.

What happens when we don't live by the Spirit?

What does the sinful nature gravitate toward?

Can you see the importance of daily choice here?

It cannot be said enough that we do have a choice. God has chosen us to be his, and now we have a choice—to live as his or to live for ourselves. He will not make that choice for us, but gives us the right to choose whom we will serve, follow, and obey. The results of following after our own flesh are disastrous!

Read Galatians 5:22-26

You've just read about the acts of the sinful nature. Now let's see what happens when the Holy Spirit is in control.

List the first three virtues listed.

Love, joy, and peace are heart-responses. They are a reflection of our relationship with God.

List the next three characteristics.

Patience, kindness, and goodness are all characteristics of the Spirit that are reflected in our relationships with others.

> We really can choose between living by the sinful nature and by the Spirit. But we can't choose the consequences. Those are fixed...God has already chosen them. What if we make this choice, and live by the power of the Spirit? Then God fills us to overflowing with love, joy, peace, patience, kindness, goodness, faithfulness, gentleness, and self-control.
>
> As the Holy Spirit flows freely in our lives, a rich and beautiful character grows. We are filled with love, with joy, with peace. In every relationship we exhibit that patience, kindness, goodness, faithfulness, gentleness, and self-control that marks us as God's own."

Lawrence O. Richards, *Devotional Commentary*, Victor Books, 2002, 967-968.

List the last three values.

Faithfulness, gentleness, and self-control are aspects of our own nature. They are a reflection of our inner self.

Did you notice that verse 22 talks about the *fruit* of the Spirit—singular and not the fruits of the Spirit—plural? We cannot pick and choose which "fruits" we want to have in our lives. Living by the Spirit means that all of these characteristics are evident. It's a package deal!

Read 1 Corinthians 12:12-27

The Apostle Paul wrote letters to the early churches to help them grow in their faith and in the understanding of God. In the New Testament we have two letters he wrote to the church in Corinth—1 Corinthians and 2 Corinthians.

What is Paul comparing the church to in these verses?

As a believer in Christ, can you choose NOT to be part of the body of Christ (v. 27)?

Ephesians 1:22-23 tells us that the church is the body of Christ and he is the head. Each believer may play a different part in the life of the church but every part is necessary and valuable. The only way you can function as part of the body of Christ is to be in relationship with other believers.

Who has arranged the parts of the body?

How does God "rank"the different parts of the body?

In verses 25-26, how are we to respond to each other in the body of Chrst?

When you get the flu, your whole body suffers–your head aches, your eyes hurt, your stomach, well, you know ... . Every part of your body suffers. It should be the same if one of our brothers and sisters in Christ is suffering. We should be so connected that we feel their suffering too. The good news is that we also get to share in their joy.

Read Colossians 3:12-17

If you want to know how NOT to behave toward others, read Colossians 3:5-11. We are going to focus on how we should act in our relationships with other believers.

Write a short definition for the following words found in verse 12:
* *Compassion—*

* *Kindness—*

- *Humility—*

- *Gentleness—*

- *Patience—*

When someone does something that hurts or grieves us, how are we to react toward that person?

What should rule over our hearts?

What actions are we to take to build up each other (vv. 16-17)?

We are to treat each other in an understanding way—making allowances for short-comings and being willing to forgive when we are wronged. Then we are to wrap up all our relationships in love. That is the way to peace and unity.

my plan

When I walk into my backyard, I see trees, shrubs and a variety of flowers and plants. As the flowers bloom in spring, and the leaves begin to bud, it is beautiful. But, as I look at the plants, I cannot see what is going on inside of them. I only see the fruit. The flowers, the buds, and the new leaves didn't happen because I went to the craft store and found flowers and leaves to glue on to my outdoor greenery. It happened naturally, as a God-given flow of life and nourishment given to the plant from the root system.

In the same way, you will grow naturally as you make the daily choice to remain connected to Jesus. How tempting it is to want immediate change. Sometimes I think we would love to go to the store and pick up a little patience and joy, slap it on with a little adhesive, and be on our way. But, that is not how the fruit of God's Spirit is born. That, my friend, would be an imitation of what is pure and true and real.

God desires to empower us, change us, and fill us with the goodness of his Spirit. Look again at what makes up the fruit of the Spirit:

- *Love*
- *Joy*
- *Peace*
- *Patience*
- *Kindness*
- *Goodness*
- *Faithfulness*
- *Gentleness*
- *Self-Control*

Do you know a Christian who is a living example to you of the fruit of the Spirit? Write his or her name here:

What can you do this week to cultivate the ground of your relationships so that the fruit of the Spirit can grow naturally?

What are you doing to grow in your understanding of what it means to be a part of the body of Christ? What else could you do?

"So in Christ we who are many form one body, and each member belongs to all the others."

Romans 12:5

Dear God,

How I thank you for supplying everything I need to grow in you. You supply the power, the guidance, the truth—everything. Now, may I learn what it means to live by the Spirit. Teach me how to be a part of your body and to relate to other believers in a way that attracts unbelievers to you. Bring to my mind each new day the importance of connecting with you and with your church.

In Jesus' Name—Amen

connecting

to God, our peace

We live in troubled times. The message of Psalm 23 is beautiful, peaceful, and stabilizing in times of trouble. But it is not just for troubled times; its message is for our everyday lives!

"The Lord is my Shepherd, I shall not want ..." is a phrase many of us know by heart. Unfortunately, somewhere in the familiarity, the power—the deeper message—has gotten overlooked or completely lost. It is a message of relationship. Truth is, Jesus is our shepherd. He is also our keeper, our helper, and the Prince of Peace. He has come to impart peace, stability and security into the lives of those who trust in Him.

In a world of chaos, each of us needs to discover peace with God. As we walk with God, it is easy to feel there is so much to learn. We can actually feel on spiritual overload! But the most important things to learn are the attributes of God that reveal his heart toward us. How can we love someone we don't know? It's all about relationship!

Recently a friend sent me the following commentary on Psalm 23 by an unknown author:

The LORD is my shepherd—THAT'S RELATIONSHIP!
I shall not want—THAT'S SUPPLY!
He maketh me to lie down in green pastures—THAT'S
    REST!
He leadeth me besides still waters—THAT'S
    REFRESHMENT!
He restoreth my soul—THAT'S HEALING!
He leadeth me in the paths of righteousness—THAT'S
    GUIDANCE!
For his name's sake—THAT'S PURPOSE!
Yea, though I walk through the valley of the shadow
    of death—THAT'S TESTING!
I will fear no evil—THAT'S PROTECTION!
For thou art with me—THAT'S FAITHFULNESS!
Thy rod and thy staff they comfort me—THAT'S
    DISCIPLINE!
Thou preparest a table before me in the presence of
    mine enemies—THAT'S HOPE!
Thou anointest my head with oil. My cup runneth
    over—THAT'S ABUNDANCE!
Surely goodness and mercy shall follow me all the
    days of my life—THAT'S BLESSING!
And I will dwell in the house of the LORD—THAT'S
    SECURITY!
Forever—THAT'S ETERNITY!

As you grow in Christ, or as you renew your commitment to Christ, there will be many things to embrace. Through it all, remember that you are developing a love relationship that will enable you to live a life of harmony and contentment regardless of your circumstances. THAT'S PEACE!

bible study

I have found that when I read a passage of Scripture out loud something wonderful happens within me. In Romans we read that faith comes from hearing the message. As I read the truth of Scripture out loud, it seems to sink in. It begins to invigorate me with faith. I am filled with a new sense of belief. I am filled with the wonder of hope! What about you?

Read Psalm 23—outloud

Write down all the things Psalm 23 says God does for you: (Example: He makes me lie down; he leads me, etc.)

Re-read Psalm 23. Give a response to each of the actions God takes: (Example: Because he makes me lie down, I will rest. Because he leads me, I will follow, etc.)

The Psalms are a collection of songs written primarily by David, the Shepherd King. About half of the 150 Psalms are known to be by David. Psalm 90 is written by Moses and Psalms 72 and 127 were written by David's son, King Solomon. The psalms are like the national hymn book of Israel. They reveal God's character and actions on behalf of his people and are intended to invoke worship and praise. Jesus was fond of the Psalms and quoted them during his ministry on earth. In fact, Jesus told us to look for him in the Psalms, even though they were written long before his birth (Luke 24:44).

Henrietta Mears, *What the Bible Is All About*, Regal Books, 1999.

How has reading Psalm 23 and personalizing
the truths touched you today? What current, personal, life
situation can be touched by relying on the truth in this Psalm?

There are two specific truths in this Psalm that have been life-changing for me. First, I accept the truth that he guides my path in steps of righteousness for his name's sake. Often my personal path does not seem righteous. Instead it seems wrought with problems. Yet I can choose to believe that in all things God is guiding me, molding me, changing me—because I belong now to him (his name's sake). What a comfort to know that God walks with us through whatever we encounter. There is no need to fear!

The second truth that encourages me is that goodness and love follow me each day. It may not seem to me like goodness is following me. But what peace of heart I can have when I believe goodness and love are following me— regardless of the circumstances surrounding me!

Read Nehemiah 9:22-28

Here we see a people God blessed. But in their humanness, they forgot the God who blessed them. All the truths in Psalm 23 were operating in their lives. Then they forgot the God of peace and turned toward their own ways again.

What was the result of the people's disobedience and rebellion? (v. 27)

God allowed the people to experience oppression until they turned their face to him again and cried out. As soon as they remembered their relationship to God, he responded with great compassion and rescued them from their enemies and returned them to his rest.

What happened next? (v. 28)

What does verse 28 show us about God's character?

God's compassion reveals a feeling of pity or distress that moves him to help or show mercy. God, in his compassionate mercy, wants us to experience his peace. We receive his peace, then look the other way and choose to live life on our own terms. Then we wonder, "Why are Christians no different? Why am I really no different? What makes the difference?"

God intends for us to be different—not perfect, but different. He wants us to be a people who embrace the truth of who he is, learn what it means to be in relationship with him, and communicate our hearts to him.

Write out the following verses and underline the truth you find in each:

- *Psalm 4:8*

- *Psalm 29:11*

- *Psalm 85:8*

- *Psalm 119:165*

Read Isaiah 9:2, 6-7

It can seem sometimes that our lives, our relationships, or the world around are full of distress, darkness, and fearful gloom. How are we to find peace in the midst of such circumstances? God has given us a gift!

Who is the gift God has sent to us?

What is he called?

This is a favorite passage for Christmas greeting cards because it tells of Jesus' birth. These are not just Hallmark platitudes! This is the absolute truth of who Jesus is on our behalf. He is the gift given to mankind, so that we can have fellowship with God.

Wonderful Counselor. He is the one who gives the right advice. Counselor comes from the Hebrew word *yaats*, which means to advise, resolve, guide, purpose. With those definitions we can say: "He is my wonderful advisor, my wonderful resolver, my wonderful guide, and my wonderful purpose!"

Mighty God. He is more than able. Mighty comes from the Hebrew word *gibbor*, which means powerful, warrior, champion, chief, giant, strong. We can now say, "He is my powerful God, a warrior, and a champion. He is my giant and strong God!"

Everlasting Father. He never changes. He is timeless. He is God our Father. Everlasting comes from the Hebrew root *ad*, which means duration, continue and advance. I can now embrace the fact that he is a father who will stay with me the duration of the journey, continuing with me throughout my lifetime. He gives me the advance—the next step.

Prince of Peace. He rules with justice and peace. Prince is from the Hebrew *sar*, which means head person, chief, captain or keeper. Peace is from the Hebrew *shalom*, which means welfare, health, prosperity and peace. Now I can say, "he is the keeper of my welfare!"

Read Matthew 1:18-23

Another Christmas card greeting? No, again this is life-changing truth. This is why we can have peace.

What name is Jesus called in verse 23?

What is the meaning of the name?

How does knowing that the Wonderful Counselor, Mighty God, Everlasting Father, and Prince of Peace is with you every minute of every day provide you peace?

Because of this new relationship with Jesus, we can embrace what is true. No longer do we have to be like the masses wandering around in distress and fearful gloom. We can, if we will embrace the truth, have peace.

What does it mean to embrace the truth? Embrace simply means: to hold closely, to accept eagerly. When embracing the truth we are holding the truth of God's Word close to us; we are accepting it as the truth it is. We are focusing on truth and building our new life on that foundation.

Read Mark 4:35-41

After a full day of ministering to others, Jesus and his followers enter a small fishing boat and set off across the Sea of Galilee. This sea is known for its unexpected and fierce storms—often occuring at night and far from shore.

Where is Jesus when the storm hits and what is he doing?

What effect do Jesus' words have on the wind and the waves?

What did Jesus ask the disciples?

These men had walked and talked with Jesus in person. They had seen him do many miracles. But even with Jesus present with them in the boat, they were overwhelmed by the storm surrounding them.

We all have doubts from time to time—but faith in the one who can save us is the source of peace even in the midst of threatening storms. Jesus can restore calm to our lives.

my plan

The *Peanuts* comic strip character Linus carries his security blanket with him wherever he goes. Sometimes the other kids make fun of him. They have tried to convince him to let go of his blanket. But Linus knows the value of peace and refuses to surrender the thing that gives him security.

What are you clinging to for security?

Read and write out the words of Christ found in John 14:27

What does he give us?

How is the peace he gives different than the peace of the world?

This verse contains a challenge. What is it?

The Amplified New Testament (Zondervan Publishing House, p. 392) says it this way—"stop allowing yourselves to be agitated and disturbed; and do not permit yourselves to be fearful *and* intimidated *and* cowardly *and* unsettled."

Peace can be fleeting. We have learned to base our peace

on money, jobs, people, circumstances—but that is the peace of the world. Real peace has been given to us by Christ. There is a bumper sticker that expresses this truth well—

Know God—Know Peace
No God—No Peace

Knowing God is an act of our minds as well as our hearts. As you continue to study his Word and receive his teachings, your relationship to him will grow and your faith in him will increase. Philippians 4:8-9 holds the key to experiencing the God of peace in your life. Underline or highlight what you will choose to focus your mind on this week:

"Finally brothers, whatever is true, whatever is noble, whatever is right, whatever is pure, whatever is lovely, whatever is admirable—if anything is excellent or praise worthy—think about such things. Whatever you have learned or received or heard from me, or seen in me—put it into practice. And the God of peace will be with you."

Dear God,

Heavenly Father, I now thank you that you are my perfect peace. May I learn to focus on what is true and not on the things around me that would rob me of peace and instill fear in my heart. In this world, I will have trouble—but I will never face it alone. You are always with me. Help me to rest in your love and provision.

In Jesus' Name—Amen

connecting
to our neighbors

S ue and Mary have lived next door to each other for
nine years. When their houses were first built, they met
often in the front yard to discuss the trials and tribulations
of home ownership. Their families worked together to develop the small plot of ground that connected their two homes.

In the early years, they exchanged cookies at Christmas
time and watched out for each others dogs and kids. In one
of their frontyard conversations, Sue learned that Mary's
brother had cancer. For many months Sue would inquire
about him whenever their paths crossed. Silently she prayed
for the family and she rejoiced when Mary announced one
day that he was in remission.

One day Sue's husband moved away and Mary discovered months later that he had left Sue and their two children
for another woman. Mary learned this from another neighbor since she rarely saw Sue anymore. Once in a while Mary
would wonder how Sue and the two children were getting
along. She meant to go over and check on her—see if there
was anything they needed. But her own life was so busy that
time slipped away until so much time had passed, she was

embarrassed now to even see Sue. So, unconsciously, she began to avoid her. Their relationship was reduced to an occasional "hi" across the fence or a wave while parking the car.

Our lives have become so busy that it's easy to excuse not being involved with people who are on the fringe of our lives. But God has called his children to something better:

> *"You are the salt of the earth ... You are the light of the world ... let your light shine before men, that they may see your good deeds and praise your Father in heaven."*

Salt doesn't do any good if it stays inside the salt shaker. And what good is a light that is hidden? God wants us to get out there and to have relationships with our neighbors, our coworkers, our acquaintances at the gym, the clerk at the grocery store and the teller at the bank.

Someone once said that you may be the only Bible some people ever read. There's a lot of truth to that. And maybe it was a Christian taking the time to be involved in your life that led you to believe in Christ. If so, then you already understand the importance of developing relationships with unbelievers.

Regardless of how long you have been saved, your relationship with Christ gives you good news to share. This study will help you understand your responsibility to your neighbors.

bible study

The question of our responsibility to love others is not a new one. Jesus was confronted by an "expert" in the law. In an effort to justify his behavior, the man asked Jesus a question—Who is my neighbor? It is a question we need to answer for ourselves.

Read Luke 10:25-37

What did the man want to know (v. 25)?

What is the answer to inheriting eternal life (v. 27)?

Why do you think the man needed to justify himself?

How did Jesus answer the question "Who is my neighbor"?

Jesus told the story of the Good Samaritan to emphasize the importance of our relationships. If we say our relationship with God is enough—we are mistaken for two reasons: (1) God has called us to be in relationship with others and (2) we cannot love God and not love others.

Read 1 John 3:16-20

How do we know what love is?

How are we to respond when we see someone in need?

It would be tempting here for us to do a little "justifying." After all, pity is a feeling of compassion. That's not hard; I can do that! How easy it is to pass a homeless person and feel genuine pity but not be moved to do anything to demonstrate the love of God to him or her. Or, to watch from the comfort of our home while the older couple across the street struggle to shovel the snow from their driveway. We think it's a shame that they have no one to help them without asking ourselves why *we* are not helping.

What responsibility are we given in verse 18?

Read Romans 13:8-10

What one continuing debt does God want us to repay?

What one rule sums up the other commandments?

Can we love others if we don't love ourselves?

The obvious answer here is "no." But what does it mean to love yourself? Perhaps you were raised in a home where any focus on self was viewed as selfish and unacceptable. Or, perhaps you grew up surrounded by criticism and ridicule. You may not even be able to identify anything lovable about yourself.

The key to loving yourself is seeing yourself as God sees you—NOT as you or anyone else sees you. This is an important first step in learning to love others.

Read Psalm 139:1-18

In your new relationship with God, you can rest in the fact that he knows you perfectly and loves you unconditionally. Accepting his perfect love allows us to love ourselves and others.

What are some of the ways in which God knows you?

How long has God known you?

How does it make you feel knowing that God knows you so intimately and still loves you so completely?

Read Luke 6:27-36

When you think about loving your neighbor, you may be thinking that it may be inconvenient, but it may not be that hard. After all, they're nice people. But God is calling us to something higher, as you will see in this passage.

Luke says that an enemy is someone who does what to you?
a)
b)
c)
d)
e)
f)

How does God expect us to respond to someone who treats us this way?

When we love our enemies and do good to them, what characterist of God are we reflecting?

How do you define mercy?

Read Luke 6:37-38

What are the two "do nots" in these verses?

What is the result to us if we do the "do nots'"

Although [mercy] means "to be greatly concerned about someone in need," it goes beyond feeling to describe compassionate treatment that addresses the need of others and acts to alleviate it.

Disciples can show mercy because God has shown it to them. The merciful are blessed because they can be assured of God's mercy.

The Bible Knowledge Key Word Study-The Gospels, Victor Books, 53.

What are the two actions we are to do? the result?

Read Matthew 25:34–40

What do these verses tell us about how God views our responsibility to our neighbors?

Is it easier or harder to give to others knowing you are really giving to God? Why?

Sometimes what we need most in our relationships with others is wisdom. God has promised to give us wisdom generously when we ask (James 1:5). Proverbs contains a lot of godly advice in choice nuggets. As you read the following Proverbs about neighbors, write down the "nugget" you discover:

Read:

- *Proverbs 3:28, 29*

- *Proverbs 11:12*

- *Proverbs 14:21*

The Book of Proverbs is a collection of sayings, intended to serve as a guide for daily life. The sayings cover many differnet topics, exploring attitudes and relationships, and evaluating such things as wealth, poverty, and power. The Proverbs reflect a kind of literature that was common in ancient times. Many of the sayings in this book were written or collected by Solomon, some 950 years before Christ. The Proverbs do not argue truth. They are short sayings that record what is without trying to explain the why or the how. They are also generalizations—certainly exceptions can be found to many of the statements. But the intent is to give us a guide of how things usually work out in the normal course of life.

Bible Teacher's Commentary, Cook Communications Ministries, 2002, 337-338.

- *Proverbs 24:28, 29*

- *Proverbs 27:10*

The bottom line is that God expects us to treat others by a standard that is different from what the world teaches. He wants our relationships with all people to be a reflection of his relationship with us—one that is loving, kind, and generous. And the only way we can do that is to stay connected to him and draw on his power.

my plan

The more connected we become to God, the more we should desire to reach out to our neighbors. If you have ever been touched by an act of kindness, then you know the profound effect it can have on the heart. As Christians, it should be our goal to demonstrate the love of God in such a way that others will be drawn to know him too.

Here are some simple steps that may help you develop a plan to show the love of God to your neighbors:

(1) Take inventory. Sometimes we do not consider helping others because we have lost sight of all that we ourselves possess. So, take some time to count your blessings. Include your possessions (house, car, clothes, pets), your relationships (family, friends, coworkers), your talents, your life lessons, your health, etc.:

1.

2.

3.

4.

5.

6.

7.

8.

9.

10.

(2) Take notice. It's hard to see much detail from the window of a speeding vehicle. If you really want to see the needs of others, you might need to slow down. Really look at the people you pass on the street or in the mall. Don't

avoid the lonely neighbor at the mailbox. Ask God to raise your "people" consciousness so that you are looking at others with eyes of love and compassion. List three people you "notice" this week that maybe you haven't noticed before:

1.
2.
3.

(3) Take action. What do you have that you could offer to another to help meet his or her need? No matter what your age, your circumstances, your current relationships, you have something you can give to help someone else. Don't be content to pity—take part! List one action you will take this week to connect with your neighbor:

Dear God,

First, I thank you for all you have given me—the many blessings in my life. Open my eyes to the needs of others. Give me a genuine love for my neighbor and light a fire within me to take part in helping those around me so that they will know the love of God in their lives.

In Jesus' name, Amen.

a final word

Remember Adam. As the first created human being, he had a perfect environment, perfect health, and perfect fellowship with God. But his aloneness was the one thing God said was not good. Enter Eve! Mankind has been connected in relationships ever since.

God is a relational being, as demonstrated in the three persons of God. We are created in his image so we get our craving for relationship—our need to belong—from him. In his book on intimacy, *Courage to Connect*, Rich Hurst says **"There is in all of us a sense of incompleteness that can only be eased when we are in relationship with other people."** Building healthy relationships is part of our journey in Christ.

God has graciously given us a road map for relationships in his Word. And he has empowered us with his presence to live in relationship. I hope that this study has helped you to understand more fully your relationship to God, and that it has given you a practical understanding of how you can live rightly in relationship to your family, your friends and neighbors, your fellow believers, and the world.